My Anxious Thoughts

Eloise du Gorrnic

ISBN 978-93-5559-234-7

Published in India 2022 by Pencil

A brand of
One Point Six Technologies Pvt. Ltd.
123, Building J2, Shram Seva Premises,
Wadala Truck Terminal, Wadala (E)
Mumbai 400037, Maharashtra, INDIA
E connect@thepencilapp.com
W www.thepencilapp.com

Author biography

Eloise du Gorrnic is a pseudonym for the real author who shall not be named for privacy purposes. Alas, the real author, or Eloise, is a young woman born in South Florida who enjoys writing about her own thoughts as well as neurobiological drug research. As her current studies and life primarily reside in Miami where many cultures and ideas collide, future writings from Eloise can include implications from her own research and from her experience with the worlds of chemistry, psychology, philosophy, and entreupreneurship. Not only does Eloise enjoy her life with research and writing, but she also loves to travel and hopes to venture to Antarctica one day to see penguins in their natural habitat.

CONTENTS

Chapter 1 Vulnerability, 02-05-18 7

Chapter 2 Addiction, 02-08-18 9

Chapter 3 The Story of Why, 02-11-18 11

Chapter 4 Poetry in its Purest Form, 02-12-18 14

Chapter 5 Desperate, 03-05-18 17

Chapter 6 Complacency, 03-18-18 21

Chapter 7 Snapshot, 04-02-18 24

Chapter 8 What, 04-02-18 26

Chapter 9 Movie, 04-23-18 27

Chapter 10 Illusion, 04-30-18 30

Chapter 11 Feeling, 05-13-18 33

Chapter 12 Love Almost, 05-15-18 36

Chapter 13 Innocence, 06-01-18 37

Chapter 14 Lost Hope, 06-08-18 39

Chapter 15 Just Maybe, 06-25-18 41

Chapter 16 Maybe Not, 07-07-18 42

Chapter 17 Touch, 07-20-18 44

Chapter 18 Unworthy, 07-23-18 45

Chapter 19 Downfall, 08-13-18 46

Chapter 20 Find Me, 08-21-18 48

Chapter 21 Hopefully, 10-10-18 50

Chapter 22 Trip, 10-25-18 52
Chapter 23 Diminished, 11-01-18 54
Chapter 24 Fear, 11-13-18 56
Chapter 25 Pearl, 11-27-18 58
Chapter 26 Unappreciated, 01-07-19 60
Chapter 27 Forbidden Love, 06-26-19 62
Chapter 28 Finished, 01-13-20 64
Chapter 29 Not Yet, 03-30-20 66
Chapter 30 I Found You, 08-17-20 68

Preface

In lieu of many anxieties during highschool, I started to write down my thoughts everytime I would get anxious. Fast forward a few years later, a simple way of getting my emotions out turned into a collection of ideas and thoughts put together in a way that not only eased my worries, but that can also aid others who may struggle with similar anxieties. In the style of poetic prose, this book was written and shared so that those who read it may feel comfort in their own lives. Not only are these writings very personal to me, they include mentions of people that I have been in love with, that I still love, and that have died. Throughout the course of the writings, the reader (you) may see some writings written to you as an audience; take these words as seriously as possible because these are my direct words and philosophies to you who may need guidance or comfort in cartain areas of your life. In no way is anyone perfect, but illusions may make even the most unworthy person as beautiful as a diamond if looked at through the right lens. Keep these things in mind while reading and always know that not everything written may apply to you, but perhaps it can teach you something new.

Chapter 1 Vulnerability, 02-05-18

2:07am

To Perfect:

I was indestructible, but then you waltzed in and made me vulnerable, and I allowed you to. Silly me I guess. But there is a strength in vulnerability —it shows your weakness, and that's all people see of you, but they don't see your strength. Hidden strength is one of the most powerful things a human can have, yet you only have it when you're vulnerable; crazy right? You don't understand, but I think about you all the time; I crave you more than I crave food when I'm hungry at times as if your attention would cease my physical pain. The truth is, I like that you're here, but it's so exhausting to know that you'll never fully be mine. Minds so alike, yet so far apart; both so beautiful, yet an angry ugliness manifests in my core, and my only explanation is you. I'm angry that you made yourself present in my life, I didn't even ask for you, but from the moment I laid eyes on you I knew that I'd cede to your control. I, an independent, strong, intelligent woman, emotionally kneels on your behalf; tell me how that works?

How someone can just creep in and disorganize every single piece of stability that is my being. The Devil himself manifests into beautiful creatures and entities, but you're not him. You're something even stronger because I somehow fell, yes I fell, for you. I hope you're honored. Only a select few have the privilege of having me like them. Although you, you little cretin, you snuck up on me and hit me in the face with yours and I couldn't help but like you. Who wouldn't like you? You're so passionate and elegant and everything about you screams love. The one problem is that I liked you, and you live hundreds of miles away from me, and you're leaving soon, and you're probably going to forget about me; I mean, I'm just one out of the countless girls in the world right? Who am I to steal all of your attention? But I fell for you, and I fell hard. The nights I've spent awake thinking about you I don't regret. All of the times I've cried over you because I knew that there was a possibility of you leaving, I don't regret those either. I don't regret them because I spent my time thinking about you; what a fool.

Chapter 2 Addiction, 02-08-18

12:43am

To Perfect:

It's almost 1am and you're the only thing on my mind. Why would God put you in my path knowing that we would fall for each other? This is the most pain I've been in since my mother died last year; I just hope there's a happy ending. You're leaving for the air force in a few months, and I'm staying here. You're leaving for four years while I have to stay and live my life without you, but the thing is that I don't want to be alone. With how I'm going to live my life, traveling the world and such until I part from this world, it's almost impossible to find someone who wants to do the same thing; but then I met you and you told me about your plans and how they somewhat aligned with mine. The only thing in our path is now: you live 150 miles from me, you're leaving for the air force for four years, and we both have uncompromising responsibilities which get in the way of us. What am I to do with you? I wish that we never met because at least if we never met I would not be crying over you because of how much I miss you and because of how brief our time will be together. In four years from now, you probably won't even remember my name, I'll simply be a face to your book of flings. I am addicted to you. Yes, I am. I think about you constantly, like how a philosopher ponders about life's meaning and how the universe was formed. You make yourself beautiful in my mind but that is all you are for now: a picture I have created in my mind. False hopes, false attitudes, false mannerisms. The only thing keeping me sane is the fact that I have to attend school 5 times a week; if not for school I would've already been in a pool of my own tears, wondering about you and wondering why you're not laying next to me asking me about life's meaning and how the universe was formed. People say heroin is addicting, tobacco is almost impossible to leave, and how meth makes you physically and mentally crave it, but I feel all of that about you. What kind of addiction are you that I lose sleep weeping about the uncertainty of our lives. What kind of addiction are you that I must grasp onto any kindness you show towards me as a reassurance that you will not leave me until the Airforce? What kind of addiction are you that when you don't respond to a text within 2 minutes I check my phone every minute or so, taking to it quickly whenever it vibrates, hoping it's you responding? I regret meeting you because I knew you'd make me go mad. If there's anything I wish I wasn't right about, it would be you and how I knew from the start you'd deteriorate me from the inside out. I'm addicted to you and I crave you every second of the day, thank you for that pleasure.

Chapter 3 The Story of Why, 02-11-18

8:45pm

<u>To Perfect:</u>

I've come to the conclusion that I love you. I thought I wasn't able to love anyone or anything truly until you came along. The fact that you're the first thought in my head every morning should be clear enough, but it isn't. The fact that I, someone who does not want to have a child, thought about having a child after our first date terminated should be clear enough, but it isn't. The fact that I've already cried over the uncertainty of our lives together five times, the most recent one being last night, should be clear enough, but it isn't. It was clear when you asked me if I loved you, even though I quickly denied my feelings, knowing that I needed a basis for my emotions. It was then, the smile on your face when you asked that silly little question, that made me fall; I knew in that moment that I never wanted to lose your smile, your excitement. I could tell that you were hoping I'd say yes, or at least a maybe, but I said no without giving any real thought to the question. I realize now that I will never find anyone as perfect for me as you are. I want to tell you that I love you next time we meet, whether it be next week or next month; I just want to see your face glow up with excitement because you know that you are wanted and that you are loved by the girl you decided to talk to at the fair that Thursday night. I think you already told me you loved me over our conversation two days ago; "eu te amo" you said, but I brushed it off, knowing that the time wasn't right, or that I imagined the words escaping from your lips. I've imagined saying the words "I love you" to you over dozens of times today and last night when I pondered about our affairs. I imagine that we are together, playing a game or watching a movie, and I just look at you and tell you that I can say a simple phrase in 5 different languages. I would say "Ich liebe dich" (German), "Je t'aime" (French), "Te amo" (Spanish), "Eu te amo" (Portuguese), and finally "I love you" (English). I've imagined your reactions, facial expressions, even the way you'd pull me in after I'd finish saying those words. I've imagined how your face would drop after I'd say the French translation, knowing that you'd recognize that phrase. As I would continue, you would only wait for me to finish with "I love you" before you could grab me passionately, and maybe say those same words back. I've fallen hard for you and you don't know why. Well, here's the explanation: after a 2 year relationship with a guy that I thought I loved, I assumed that I never had the ability to ever love anyone. I broke up with him after 2 years of "loving" him, but instead of heartbreak and despair I felt relief. I felt a stupidity in my being for wasting 2 years of my adolescence with someone who only wanted me for my body and my abilities. When my Junior year of high school started, I was surprised to find out that this boy I had paid close attention to the year prior was in two of my classes, one in which where he sits directly next to me. I began to grow feelings for him, even though nothing was there. This boy is pale, he is a jerk, and he would never give me any special attention, but I grew feelings. It's strange how the human mind works; it craves what it doesn't have and discards what it can easily obtain. My "crush" on him got so bad that one day I drank to forget my feelings about him instead of crying; the moment you cry over a boy it better be serious because no boy will ever deserve your painful, angelic tears. I made a vow to myself around Christmas-time that I would not have any stupid crushes or any boyfriends in the year 2018. I met you two mere days after Christmas thinking that God was playing some sick joke on me, presenting me with a beautiful boy mere days after my vow. After the winter break, I went on a missions trip to Mexico with my Junior class (I had already been on two dates with you), and all of my feelings for the boy who sits next to me had escaped and gotten lost in the wind; I thought of you every single day, and I still do. Moral of the story: you pieced together a heart that was incapable of true, unconditional love, by simply entering my life. I don't know why I feel this way about you, considering the fact that I've only been on two dates with you and we haven't seen each other since New Years, but I do know that there is a reason why you entered my life and my heart. With our given circumstances, I don't know if you'll break what you have pieced together or if you'll keep it bandaged. All I know for now is that I love you and that you might as well be the most wonderful mistake I've ever allowed to enter my heart.

Chapter 4 Poetry in its Purest Form, 02-12-18

12:00am

To Me:

I analyze poetry and I ponder about life's meaning with many people and many differing elements, but I myself spew poetic genius when I cry and when I feel like I have no control over my life. My own weakness and instability brings about the purest and most poetic form of bluntness. My own weakness makes me not care about others' emotions or whether I'll be able to cope with the situation at hand, but I do know that somehow I will overcome it. As I listen to songs to cope with my emotions for Perfect, and as I drink to feel numb to my feelings for a brief, glorious moment, I can't help but to ponder whether my reactions matter at all. Does it ever matter? Whether I can't sleep at night because I can't stop thinking about Perfect or if I sleep peacefully without a care to the world around me? I hope it does matter, because my tear stains and my worrying cannot be in vain; my emotions cannot be taken lightly. Poetry in its purest form is one that comes at a spur rather than at deep thought and meticulous studying. Poetry is in all of us, whether it be in physical activities, in words, in facial expressions, or in mere thoughts. Poetry is the product of humanity's desire and need to make sense of the world, even if metaphors and allusions are made to make sense of the unknown emotions. Our lives swim away into oblivion and all we can do is think and react for our time here on earth. Human history dates back about 7000 years; imagine all of the history and emotions lost to the sea of forbidden knowledge. Imagine all of the great generations of warriors and kings and queens and skilled workmen who have been forgotten about. Of course our brain capacity would never be able to even imagine the full impact of that statement, but I can't help but wonder if I'll be forgotten about too. People often ask what my greatest fear is. They often assume that I fear snakes, sharks, heights, or even little spiders, but my greatest fear isn't so shallow. My greatest fear is not something tangible, rather it is something that cannot be controlled or even reached; you never know when it could strike. Oblivion is my greatest fear and I fear it more than I fear losing another loved one. I cannot be alive and have my history erased from the memories of those who deserve to hear my story. I am a mere human but I do not want to be forgotten like the poor nameless corpses of the Holocaust or like the victims of murderers. Our lives are so short and we waste everyday with temporary thoughts and whims, not knowing when we can part from this world. Carpe Diem they say, Seize the Day. It seems empowering at first but as time passes you lose sight of its meaning; I've done this many times myself and I hate the feeling of knowing that I've wasted an entire 24 hours of my ever so fleeting life to lethargy. I am alive right now. At this moment I have not parted from the world; think about that for a while. One day you will die but today you are alive on Earth to do whatever your heart desires. Take that risk, it won't matter after you die. Take that opportunity even if it seems difficult, it can only help you grow. Don't take negativity; you have one life, do not for God's sake spend it depressed in a locked room. I am not an optimist or a pessimist, I simply see the world as an infinite poem with which death and life coexist together in its purest form. How you live your life is your choice, do not let anyone tell you otherwise; not your parents, not your teachers, not your friends, not your responsibilities. Life is yours, you have one and one only, make it the best and longest possible. Seek poetry within yourself, whether it be in your tears or in your laughter or in your fears. Learn from your mistakes and do not take everything so personally. Seek your purest form and run to it, there is no other like it.

Chapter 5 Desperate, 03-05-18

12:07am

To You:

You would think that I have a mental disease, in which I do. I don't know how to explain it, like many other things, but I've always known it even if the doctors didn't. I linger and I wander endlessly in my thoughts about today and tomorrow and next week and next year and the next decade up until my death. I have my life planned out, but does it have plans for me? I consider myself of higher intelligence; I can understand the mind process of many without even knowing them at times. I can perceive things from an animal's point of view even though I am not an animal; I promise I'm not a psychopath. I am something else. I am desperate and I am here. Desperate is such a strong word for me considering that I am autonomous and that many find it hard to enter my path as do I in theirs. I have few close friends and yes I tell them mostly everything about my life, but I cannot trust them entirely. I have not found anyone I can truly trust my life with other than God; humans are as faulty as their creations. Limited and ugly. I do not strive for greatness and I do not care either, I just want to be happy in this awful world. I wonder why I was born or why I choose, or routinely, brush my teeth first thing in the morning or after a shower. I did not choose to live in Florida, I was born and raised there. I did not choose my dad or his disgraceful actions, but I still have him. I did not choose to be of Brazilian descent, yet here I am speaking fluent Portuguese, with most of my family in Brazil. The concept of this world is so limited, how can anyone not believe in God? There lies an entire world beyond our universe that we do not know of and it is infinite. To our little human minds infinity cannot truly be represented, but think of a day that never ends: years pass, decades, generations, milleniums, and so on and so forth. It will not stop, it will not cease, it continues. At least on Earth I know that I will eventually sleep and that I will eventually die. But what about after death? Nothing? Like the supposed nothing that started all of humanity and Earth and the universe? Excuse me but are you really thinking??? You claim that an infinite universe exists from a poof, yes a poof that contradicts all of your laws of science and physics, but an infinite being seems too "out of proportion" right? Where do you think we get morals or the ability to love or how we know how to smile even if we are born blind and we cannot bear witness to an expression of joy? It is ingrained in our beings. Try to contradict me if you will but I am not wrong. Really think though it: where is your purpose in life? To be a doctor, an accountant, a salesman, a common worker? I doubt that any of you are truly happy in your office jobs, I myself couldn't bear a day sitting in front of a computer doing math or on the phone with clients all day with a 9-5 schedule; it's not natural to be sitting that long and dormant. I cannot understand why or how racism became or is a thing of "power", parallelism even. Ancient Egyptians had Hebrew slaves and the Romans captured anyone they wanted to to become their servant. It began there: the notion that I, a human, am more powerful than you, another human, because I allow myself to shut off my own emotions to torture another human for my own pleasure; and they allow me to because I am scary and they don't want to die under my hands. Or they are too nice to say no, or they know that they have no other way in life other than serving me into their lengthy demise. And racism, why? Why hate someone else for their skin or nationality; they didn't choose it and neither did you choose your own. There are more important things in your life than your Ego, whatever that may mean to you. I am so fed up with the social racism and the protests and the fights. I want it to end and I want to be happy, but of course no one in this world thinks exactly like me so none of this change can happen unless you choose it for your own. One of my favorite songs is "Man in the Mirror" by Michael Jackson, and the two lines which make it my favorite are "If you want to make the world a better place/ Take a look at yourself, and then make a change". Change starts with you. The butterfly effect exists, and every action that we take cannot be erased so please choose your life wisely. Your one act of kindness or non-hatred could change nations. What if you were conceived a day later? Your entire history would change as well as your friends and your circumstances because of a DAY. I once saw a post about a man who committed suicide and later in his house the police found a note which read "if someone smiles at me today, I will not jump". If one person, only one out of the thousands he probably encountered that day, were to just look at him and flex the mere 17 muscles needed to smile, he would not have jumped and I would not be writing about his story right now. If I had just called my friend when I thought of calling him last August I could have prevented his suicide. I cannot erase my actions and you cannot erase yours, but as the saying goes, "everyday is a new day". You do not need to wait until 12am or when you wake up to redo your day, you can start it after you had a bad day or after you had a fight with a loved one. You were given a mind, a body, and a soul; what you do with it is your choice. Oh, and don't be hard on yourself, it only makes the circumstance worse. Understand that you are human and that mistakes happen; we are the essence of mess-ups and tragedy. Yes, I am desperate and I might be a little crazy, but I am desperate and crazy for change. I can't convince you any more to change your bad ways, but I can remind you that life is yours and that you do not need to suffer and wait any longer.

Chapter 6 Complacency, 03-18-18

11:32pm

To Me:

I have a complacency for my apathy. It's a talent like no other. The way that I move from one to another without regrets, without feeling. Feeling, I feel nothing and I guess it adds a smudge to my heart and in my morals but I can't help it. I crave to be the best at my apathy, my ability to not be shattered, like a bulletproof window. You can try to hurt me, you can try to smash me to the ground and into ashes, but I don't allow you to and that is my strength. Feelings are okay, feelings are what keep good people good and what keep lovers together, but I can't feel anymore. I may be happy and sad at times, like everyone else, but a part of me in every situation whispers "but why should I care, why does it matter". Maybe that's why I thought about suicide in its depths so often, what does it matter to me? Would I even feel anything? Would I actually see a bright light? But I always stopped because I knew that Heaven would not be awaiting me if I did so, murdering myself is a sin after all; only God can determine life and death but some people really push their limits. Never blame God for reckless and senseless killings and massacres; yes He is in control but He also gave us control over ourselves, and who's to say that we're perfect in every way? We can't determine the future accurately. Why live then if everything is spontaneous? Stability in routine right? Well not me. Carpe Diem and all that jazz, and I adore such practices of destroying a confining situation, but again why? Why seize the day? Does it really matter? Why am I here? Why am I trying this? I should be doing homework, but again what does it matter if I will die someday, or even tomorrow, I don't know my fate. This is why carpe diem. Take everyday like it's your last and you won't regret your being, and why not leave a story for others to tell after you've passed? Be a legacy. I adore my ability of complacency because with it I can conquer and not care, I can walk in confidence and not think twice about if someone looked at me the wrong way; what do I care anyways? I am me and I am beautiful. My life is mine, I shouldn't be trying to please others if they exploit me for my own pleasantness. Life is mine and I shall seize it like loot from a lost paradise, taking it all and claiming it all as mine, even though the components are not all "mine" to be exact. I walk in strength but in reality I walk in apathy; I just can't find a plausible argument for putting my effort of emotions into mortal things, they flee. Don't catch anything that keeps flying away, you'll tire yourself out and wonder why you were chasing it in the first place. Life is a constant circle of wondering, pursuing, conquering, and losing; but you must remember that life could end at any of these points. Why care at all, I reiterate? Why chase? Why want? Why lose it in the end? The adrenaline rush?

The longing for love? I have a complacency for my self esteem, it can only rise. Try to lower it, I dare you, I'll lower yours even farther. Again, my apathy gets in the way, sorry I guess. People call it blunt or rude, I call it coping. Coping with the disasters at my feet and coping with the constant battle in my mind about everything, yes everything. I long for a rest, I long for peace, and I long for happiness, but where is it? If it doesn't find me I'll never find it, I know that I can live without it. If you've been a day without something or someone, trust me you can go many more days without it. One day is a start, one day could be your legacy, one day you will find it, but I hope that you don't lose sight through emotions. "Go with the flow" as they say, and never get stuck.

Chapter 7 Snapshot, 04-02-18

12:28am

To Me:

I am here. I am now. Let me preserve this innocent being; I can only obtain more knowledge of the horrors of this world with each new second. I have my youth until it has passed. One day I won't even remember what it felt like to have a flat stomach or to have soft skin. Take pictures, write down your thoughts, keep personal documents. You never know when historians in the next years to come could use your documents to describe this era, this part of you and of your life that you chose to remember. Share stories, make stories for people to remember you by; true pain comes when you are forgotten about: unloved and unwanted. My heart breaks for those who could not leave a legacy. Do we know all of the names of the Pompeii victims? Or a name of any of the minor spartan warriors? Or the name of the first man to jump off of a bridge? We don't. They didn't leave a profound legacy. One day George Washington and King Henry VIII will be forgotten about, but their documents will remain and they will be taught again. Make yourself known and always write down your feelings, what's the worst that could happen anyways? Didn't Anne Frank risk her life by writing down where she was hiding and who hid her in her diary? Some people's emotions are harder to find than nuclear launch codes: only a select 2 or 3 can really know them without a big "boom" happening. Make yourself vulnerable for your own sake. A silver bullet can't destroy your shield with one hit; rebuild yourself and grow. Write a letter to yourself in a year, 5 years, maybe even in 20 years; you can look back at how naive you were and how you never knew that your life could be changed in so many ways. Last year, I thought that I was going to marry my boyfriend at the time, and my mother would be present, watching me walk down the aisle. Little would I know that the next week she would pass and that I would break up with that boyfriend in July. I cannot be stuck in my past: life moves on even if I don't. That's all I kept thinking as I mourned over my mother in the first few days: " life moves on, things will get better, but it is okay to feel like this now." And now here I am. 17, with my plans of traveling the world and writing many books and owning a pirate ship by the time I'm 45. I have big dreams and I dare to write them down. I know about change, and I know about life's unpredictability, but will I veer from my true ambitions?

Chapter 8 What, 04-02-18

1:57am

To Me:

What exactly are you waiting for?

Chapter 9 Movie, 04-23-18

7:03pm

To Me:

It's in times like these that I feel like I'm in a movie; when I look back at old pictures and reminisce on the "good old days"; when I look into the eyes of the deceased in my old picture gallery on my laptop; while listening to my sad playlist all with the intention of being able to live like how I used to. It wasn't perfect, it never was, but at least I had my mother. I think: how did everything change so fast? Is it when she perished? I think so. I remember after she passed all I could think was "am I even alive? Am I in a coma?". The concept of the area of the universe could be easier to explain to me than it was for me to understand that she had passed. I was in utter disbelief and utter shock when my father told me the news. I could remember her in the hospital bed the day before; I could remember her picking me up from school in her white minivan not even 6 months earlier. I could remember her warm smile and I can still remember how her hands felt when I touched them: bony and clammed but filled with love. I remember looking on her left hand and seeing her engagement ring under her wedding band. I remember the way she would put on her makeup before church and how she would do her eyeliner: on her waterline. I remember that old brown cardigan-sweater thing she would wear just about everyday. I remember her wig that she would put on and be embarrassed about. I remember her lighting up when her hair grew long enough so that she wouldn't have to wear that itchy wig anymore. I remember the taste of her homemade chicken pie, so juicy and the crust so crumbly, and I remember how she would make it, each step ingrained in my brain. I remember that one time she made scorching hot sweet milk for me to drink when I was very sick at home. I remember her laugh, the joy in her eyes and the crinkles by her eyes as she would smile. Oh that smile, if I could just see it one more time. Oh that laugh, if I could just hear it one more time. Oh her hugs, if I could just have one more I would never let go. I write these sentences as tears stream down my face and as I can barely see what I am typing, If my life were a movie I could just rewind and live like I did in the past on a constant replay. If I could just see her one more time. If I could just be a toddler again and not have to worry about growing up or my next deadline or how the government could potentially risk my life. I want my innocence back. With every good movie there is an ending. With every good movie there is at least one conflict. This is not my first nor my last. Like a good movie you don't know when the ending scene will appear, you watch it with full attention until the credit reel comes, and then you get sad when you realize that the movie has ended. I love the movies that have extra clips after the credit reel, like an extra bit of enjoyment before you return to the actuality of reality. A movie cannot be infinite; it cannot simply for the fact that people will get bored of it. We as mortal beings like mortal things, such as money and power, the two most fulfilling and fleeting things on this planet. We cannot understand the immortal, like the concept of love and God. Those immortal things are what matter the most and yet we look past them because they are "boring" or are "too much to handle". If only I wasn't mortal and I could have an everlasting movie.

Chapter 10 Illusion, 04-30-18

9:10pm

To Perfect:

I've come to the conclusion that you are not what I made you to be. The time we spent apart, those four long months before April 21st, I made you to be wonderful. You are a reminder to me that I simply cannot feel. Yes I have my moments, and yes I do cry and get overwhelmed at times and at other times I rejoice with happiness; but I cannot feel. I am numb to love I guess, whatever that may mean, whatever I pictured us to be. You told me yourself that Sunday afternoon before you dropped me off at home that we live too far for anything to happen which requires commitment, that you'd be leaving for the Airforce soon and that we simply cannot be together. I will still see you for my prom in a few weeks, hopefully, but life is so unsure and I don't know if I want you anymore. You put in no effort to talk to me and you simply do not have the energy to keep a conversation. You make me look like a fool for once loving you, or whatever illusion I was caught up in. I find myself still piecing together how we could maybe be together and work out, but then I remember that life is full of uncertainties and that I am numb to love, romantic love that is. I might not be numb, I could just be in waiting for it to come, but for now I do not feel for you or any other morsel of the male gender. I lay in my bed still thinking about our time at that French restaurant and how delicious those desserts were later that night. I still dream that it could've went better, for my own sake. I wanted everything to be perfect for the one night, but alas life strikes again with its unexpectedness. I feel bound to these memories as they fade from my recollection. I miss you, but I do not need you. I enjoy your presence, but its not what makes me the happiest. I made us to be this unrealistic illusion in my mind and I absolutely hate that the illusory version of you is better than your actual self, but alas all humans have flaws. I need myself right now and if you feel like entering my life you must knock; I don't want to knock on your door anymore and hope that you'll open to let me in. I'm not crushed by this realization, I am simply just numb in my pondering. I am young and I should not put such an importance on this one, little thing: my romantic life. In the perspective of an evolutionist, they could say that I am ready to "spread my genetics" or whatever way they want to express reproduction, but have they counted in the fact that I do not want children? I maybe want one at most just to see what half of my DNA would look like growing up, but is it really necessary? Overpopulation is an issue right now and I love that in a way I am helping solve that problem by not wanting 3 or 4 children like others, but does that lessen my worth? It doesn't. It's strange how much I romanticized you. I thought that maybe I would enjoy having a child if it were with you, but now I see that once again it was just my mind filling in empty gaps with happy placebo glue. I keep thinking, why would God let you meet me if I explicitly asked not to be with anyone in 2018, I did not want another emotional train running though my limbic system. I met you and it was probably a lucky mistake that you entered my life, but all things have their end. Whether we end it next month or when you leave for the Airforce, it will end. There are no guarantees in life except endings, one of which being death. You like me a lot, and I know that, I've seen how much you care for my small details and how you take care of me, but a part of me screams "NO" everytime I think about you. Tell me why that is, that I do not want you? Oh wait, I did not want you in the beginning so why does it matter now? Claim me before you lose me, because once you lose me I'm lost from you forever. Knock on my door before I move to a bigger and better house.

Chapter 11 Feeling, 05-13-18

9:28pm

To Perfect:

I don't know why I feel this way about you, the apathy, yet a part of me still wants you. Maybe your attention, maybe my longing for love, maybe a part of me wants to be happy, but you are not it, and yet my heart veers towards you. I found myself today missing your presence, missing our times together and the way that you look into my eyes, but again you are not what I want. Everything in me knows that I deserve better, that you will not complete me, but I again still focus on you. I don’t want to feel this way, especially since you really don’t talk to me. I might just be caught up in the fact that I may never find anyone to settle with, given the circumstances of my future plans of being an international nomad. Perhaps a part of me wants what everybody else has: a person. Not just a regular person, but a person that I can hold onto when all else fails, someone who will inevitably resolve a situation that I may find impossible, just somebody to look after me. Today is Mothers Day and I almost cried at work when a coworker asked me if I had already wished my mother a Happy Mother's Day. All I could reply with was "I guess you don't know, I don't expect you to know but she passed away over a year ago". I felt so helpless in that moment, in a room full of mothers all looking at me like an orphaned duckling. I shed tears right now at the recollection of that moment, the tears that I held back, that I fought back rather. A whole restaurant full of mothers and some with their children and families, others with their group of friends, and I without one to call my own. My mother would be proud of the woman that I became after her passing, I don't doubt it, I've grown so much. My father and I were talking today and it was probably the first time that he realized that I will be turning 18 years old in 5 months, 5 short months; it's pretty shocking to think that I am so close to adulthood in the American perspective. I say these things because a part of me wants the security that I once had when I had my mother present, a part of me wants to be taken care of despite my unwillingness to cede to any authority. My own independence is a weakness in many ways, I get in people's way and disrupt their lives because I have to do something my way. I could be stubborn, or I could be a faster thinker and worker, I don't know, but I do know that I do not work well around people. This is why I say that I most likely will not have a life partner, I myself do not allow it through who I am; I wish that I could change a little portion of that about myself. I crave alone time so that I can think properly and do what I want to do rather than doing what people desire of me, but I do not like being alone. I am an extrovert and I crave attention and I yearn for love, but I do not know if I will find it. You are the closest thing I have found yet to being “the one”, but I guess it’s all a guise. I know that we will not get anywhere far, but I still want you, as crazy as it seems. I probably sound crazy, and you probably do not want me in the way that I want you. Your sweet words are mere aimless whispers to my ears; they fade quickly. Our memories, however, I can recollect them vividly and in order, as if a movie were playing in my head. I cringe at the love publicized by social media and couples in the streets, yet I want a bit of it for myself. Am I crazy for wanting something that I know will tear me apart? Am I so bad of a person that I shy away from you? Perhaps.

Chapter 12 Love Almost, 05-15-18

7:00pm

To Perfect:

No matter where you are, you will always hold a special place in my heart.

Chapter 13 Innocence, 06-01-18

10:52pm

To Me:

I lay here in an apathetic nuance not knowing what will become of my life. I feel like I've somehow thrown all of my good days away and only bad ones await me. I can only live today once, and I wonder if I lived it to its full potential. I feel like I have made a mistake, just maybe. I do not want to lead him down a dark path. Somehow, I have become the opposite of what most anyone thinks of me: innocent. I've seen and done too many things to be surprised anymore. I lay here in wonder of my opposition, who or what it could be. I wonder if it follows me, if it stalks from a distance or if it hides in plain sight. I will probably never find out who or what seeks my demise, but all I know is that it exists. I've become satisfied with many things, but nothing feels whole. Am I broken? Am I lost? My times of innocence have passed and I have grown into a woman who stands up for herself and who knows the difference between love and lust. I am here on earth and alive and the most worth that I can conjure up is my own self-built worth. I possess little wealth and I may be lost at times, but I know who I am and that separates me from the vast majority. I want to leave a legacy, but what kind?

Chapter 14 Lost Hope, 06-08-18

12:44am

To Me:

I just want to float endlessly. I don't care where I float to, I just want to float and not have to care about anything anymore. Life is so short and I can't live it with regrets. Why must I act this way? Why am I sitting in a Walmart parking lot writing this chapter? Why do I still hold onto my dear friend when all he does is ignore me? I feel so worthless. I have one life and I live it with the feeling of unworthiness. Is it so hard to live a good life? I hope my goals are achievable. I want to lay down and never have to rise up. A peaceful rest, an endless sleep. Not death itself, but a rest. Life doesn't seem real anymore, especially when I do regrettable things without feeling regret. I have this hole in my heart that will probably never be patched up or fixed, whatever can be salvaged of my heart that is. I feel like all hope is lost, lost in some intricate forest with wormholes and mirrors; it just makes it harder to be found. Hope exists, but it is lost to me, I must find it. I almost cried today at my friends betrayal, he doesn't know how much he's hurting me by not doing anything about our friendship, or whatever remains of it. I thought he cared about me, but I guess not. He is just a gust of wind in my life but I wanted him to be an oak tree, and that was my mistake.

Chapter 15 Just Maybe, 06-25-18

8:19am

To Tchutchuco:

If we do get married, just know that I knew we were destined for it since this moment; I've never felt a stronger connection with anyone else. I might just love you.

Chapter 16 Maybe Not, 07-07-18

12:43am

To Me:

I don't really think I'm made for anyone. I can be a part of someone's life for a time, maybe a moment, but it won't be anything more than that. "I'm still young", I tell myself, "You just haven't found the one yet", I continue. I long for a passionate love story yet I solely act upon flirtatious affairs. Am I sabotaging my own love story? I don't want to. I try to remain faithful to whatever current fling I associate myself with, as if they are worth my time, but I cannot separate myself and wait for my true love to make himself known to my conscience. My aspiration in life is to be happy, and I believe that involves a certain man in my life. Once I attach, it is difficult to unattach, but it does not hurt. I know that there must be a reason for the separation, perhaps a life lesson or a reminder of my past, or that I am simply destined for greater things, "greater expectations". Words seem to jumble into incoherent sounds once thought about profusely; I hope that I have the opposite effect on my future husband. With more time and thought passing, I want to be his main interest, as humbly as possible. I want to be the reason why that person wakes up in the morning: to be able to see my face and to cherish me. I hope that I'm not asking for too much, I simply want what I define as happiness to myself: to be adored by the one person that matters most to me. I don't want to be alone, I simply want a filling and happy life, but let's see where life takes me with my unending conscious adventures of the future.

Chapter 17 Touch, 07-20-18

6:11am

To Mô Linda:

I hate that you're just a mere memory; your smile, your laugh, your gaze, your hugs, your kisses: all moments in time in which I would do most anything to get back. In this moment, I become frail at our moments together. I miss you so much. It's almost difficult to believe that you were once alive; I've been so accustomed to your absence that I forget that you are my mother. My heart aches for you. I shed tears because I no longer have or will ever have your touch again. I keep your perfumes atop of my vanity yet I do not take a whiff in your remembrance; I guess it's too much to bear. I love you so much and you will never leave my conscious, mô linda.

Chapter 18 Unworthy, 07-23-18

6:34pm

To Tchutchuco:

You're not worth it. My time, my thoughts, my efforts all mean nothing to you and that is all you are going to be: a moment in time, a thought, a tiny effort, nothing more. I really thought that you were different, but you're just like the rest. I don't know why I tried. You've failed me and my expectations of a gentleman. You are nothing more than the dust in the air and I put you at a high importance to my life. I should've known better, I should've trusted less. You could've just been having a bad day, but why hurt me with your words? I'm too young to know for sure whether or not I'll be married in the years to come, all I know is that it's not you. Put value in what you want to grow; I did that but all you did was flatten. Mon cœur me fait mal pour toi, et tu est la raison.

Chapter 19 Downfall, 08-13-18

10:12pm

To Me:

It's the end of an era, I don't know how to feel. I've peaked and now I'm descending. Life is halfway figured out and even though I just started, it feels like I can't do any better than I've already done. My era of greatness has ended, all that awaits now are the rewards. But I don't want anything from past accomplishments; I want to be awarded according to my performance. I feel like I've had it too easy; I might've had it well but now is the time that I fight for what's mine. I cannot stay dormant, I cannot stay in one place, I have to move around, I must. People love comfort but I cannot feel comfortable when there is too much peace, nothing is truly peaceful after a war. I have lies to uncover, hopefully not soon. I hide too much and it hurts me, and only me, yet I continue to repeat my actions. I wonder "who am I?", as if there's an actual answer. I need to figure myself out for my well being and the well-being of others. I cannot hide anymore, I've been dormant for too long. I must fight, solitude is only a strength when you reap its rewards, not when you've hit rock bottom and you think "I can only rise at this point". How tragic to think like that, that you are at your worst. You don't know you're at your worst until you perish, and you haven't even had the time to ponder about your worst moment in life. I know that I will hit this "worst" soon, I can just feel it, it might become an entire book in the near future, I just hope that I'm prepared for my worst. I don't want to die.

Chapter 20 Find Me, 08-21-18

12:01am

To The One:

I'm in love and I don't know with whom. I'm in a maze and just when I thought I had my path figured out, it ended up being a dead end, so I had to backtrack and go into another path. I don't like this feeling: the need for a man, a yearning for a love that I don't have. It's haunting to feel so lonely even when there are people around me who love me, even people who I meet for the first time shower me with their loving words and kindness. My hormones are crazy and I guess it's because of how fast I'm maturing; my body probably thinks that I'm ready to have a baby or something and that I need a man, even though I know that I do not. I do not need a man, but my want is so strong that "need" seems to fit the description more than a temporary fix. I want a lasting relationship, but who wants the same with me? I'm so crazy and spontaneous and intelligent, I just scare them away. I can get my way if I want it bad enough, yet I lean back and let life make the decisions for me. I want control back, but I know that life will fall into place if I do my part. I want a nice, strong man to protect me. I want him to be handsome and charming and in every way masculine. I want a lover to keep forever, even if there are tough times in between now and the end of time. I need a comforter for when I get anxious or melancholy. I need a forever companion who I can trust more than a best friend. I need him to always smell like he just left the perfume department at Macy's. I want hair that I can tug and mess around with. I need a strong build to protect me and to be able to hold me back when I feel like life is falling apart. I need you, whoever you are, to reveal yourself to me soon, before I turn back to my old ways and lose yet another opportunity at love. Please run quick to me before it's too late. Don't be afraid. If you feel like it's "love at first sight", it's because it was meant to be; how many other opportunities are you going to have to immediately fall in love with someone's eyes? Just run, sprint, fly like a falcon if you can, just don't hesitate. I love you, whoever you are, wherever you may be, and whenever you find me.

Chapter 21 Hopefully, 10-10-18

1:13am

To Perfect:

I confessed my love for you today, as I intended to do since last night when you accidentally slipped up on the phone and said "love you" before hanging up. I imagined the words coming out passionately, but they instead came out of relief and surprise. We had a nasty argument, one of which could have been avoided very easily by me not making such a big deal out of the situation, but I however did. You did the right thing in the end and walked out of the restaurant and walked to where your car was parked, half a mile away. I don't blame you, I would've done the same thing, I too am human. I stayed back, feeling proud of myself, but when I moved my step I felt compelled to go after you; I thought to myself "why should I? I've wanted to drop him so long ago and now is my chance to get rid of him and the feelings", yet I also thought "why did I obsess and think about him all day today and even imagine the moment when I would be confessing my love to him?" It was then that I knew that I truly loved you;

when I broke through my pride to humble myself and fight for you back. We had a lengthy discussion, which led to tears streaking down my face. You humbly told me that you loved me, and continued saying a few other words. It was then that I knew and felt that the time was right; "I fucking love you too" escaped my trembling lips. I never imagined that love could be so painful and so beautiful at the same time. I also never imagined that I would have had to say those words after a heated argument. I read chapter 3 to you, with a shaky voice and tears blocking my view; you absolutely loved and understood why. I love you, please don't make me regret chasing after you.

Chapter 22 Trip, 10-25-18

1:53am

<u>To Him:</u>

You tripped in front of me a few hours ago, right before we entered the Miami office for our work. I told God that I would turn from my old ways, and I asked that the next boy that falls in front of my feet will be the one I marry. Is it you? I would tell myself repeatedly "I am going to marry …", and after a while it faded, but something occurred that made me want to return saying it. I told myself that a boy falling in front of my feet was probably the clearest sign that I could've ever received from God Himself, but something in me fears if the trip was brought up by another force. I loved spending time with you tonight; you always know how to put me in a good mood, I hope that I do the same for you. I saw your face as I did a cheek-kiss greeting to a new representative at the Miami office, first at the office itself, then at a sports bar before we left. I told myself that you don't want anything with me, that you might consider me a sister rather than a lover or even a wife. I could be imagining all of this, illusory correlation and all of its entities, but I can't help but wonder if it is true: that we will be joined as one flesh. You are the purest man to have been around me as a friend; I feel a cleansing everytime we decide to do something together. Again, I could be overthinking all of this. I mean, what would you want to do with me? I set myself too low, hopefully you can take me as I am. My mind constantly swirls at the thought of you, my darling, wonderful one. Grasp tightly to me, and don't let me go.

Chapter 23 Diminished, 11-01-18

7:50pm

To Me:

I am an absolute nobody. I'm unable to make money on my own anymore, all I do is screw up situations for myself, and I feel so unappreciated. I just want to let go. It's interesting how when you cry tears of anguish you can feel the pressure build in your tear ducts before being released. "I want to sink/ I want to cease/ I want my end to be my demise". I wrote that for Stoneman Douglas earlier this year in a poem, but now I use those same words to describe a different pain. I feel so useless in this world, as if my bright light was dimmed to a mere speck in the dark. I don't feel special, I feel like I've ruined my life already. All I do is mess up. I have no self control whatsoever and my desire to grow has diminished. I want to feel special again, to feel important, to feel unconditionally loved. Logically, I know that I have those, but I don't feel it anymore. I've lost my sensitivity and now all these emotions run through my veins. I want it to end quickly, I don't like this feeling. Help me, please. I want to get away, live my own life, not one predestined or pre-planned. I want a spontaneous adventure with all the repercussions. I want to feel alive. I've lost my sense of purpose, I need to find it again. I don't even know where to start. Should I not speak to anyone for days? I don't know. I try so hard to imagine a future in every decision that I make, but why put in so much effort? Why am I writing right now? It eases my pain, that's why. Uncertainty hurts more than certainty to me. That's why it's so difficult to process my own mistakes, I don't see the results as a problem. I must find a solution. I want no help. I must do this on my own. Help me.

Chapter 24 Fear, 11-13-18

8:32pm

To Me:

To be passionate about something is to find it in everything: clothing, nature, structure, reactions. I think about you in this way; a little bit of everything reminds me of you. I also think about psychology in this way. Am I passionate? I don't want to say obsessive, but it could act as a part of me, my personality. I ponder about motives and reactions incessantly, as if to make sense of the world and my own sanity. Belief itself bases itself through "nature vs. nurture" and how one's personality interacts with the belief. Passion is powerful, and so is fear. Passion explodes through caged walls and confining barriers. Fear provokes passion into a ritual rather than an adventurous opportunity, a dream realized. Fear confines and motivates us: the fear of dying keeps us alive, a fear of losing promotes a competitive spirit, a fear of oblivion creates a desire to live life to its fullest and succeed. Fear, the true motive, confines and drives passion; without a fear of not reaching one's goals and aspirations, modern life would not exist. Fear strengthens, but fear confines. Do not become a recluse.

Chapter 25 Pearl, 11-27-18

2:06am

To Him:

All I want in life is happiness, it's my aspiration. I needed to remind myself of that just now, after hours of making up conversations between us that may or may never occur. I'm smitten, completely, and I can't let you go. I feel stupid almost, considering your betrayal Friday night. I waited 30 minutes for you, and you never showed; not even a text sent to explain why. 12 hours later you respond that you were asleep. Imagine the hurt, the anger, the betrayal. I'm merely a pearl cast upon swine; precious, yet invaluable to those who do not and can not recognize it's worth. For half of my drive home that night I cried and wondered why I let myself get so close to you, how you didn't see my worth. I still think about that now, how invaluable I must be to you for us not to say a word to each other since then. I can't say that I loved you, but you definitely left your mark; it's my job now to remove it. I can't help but think why God would make it so clear that we would marry if I were to feel like this soon after that sign? I crave attention, yours especially, but something in me resents you. I've only recently in the past few hours felt like starting a conversation with you, but why read the same book over and over again and expect a different ending? I have much faith and hope, but you make it so difficult to believe that marriage is God's plan for us. Overthinking only leads to harm and I guess that's where I stand, on the brink of despair. I don't blame you for my feelings, but you do have a large impact on them. If only you knew.

Chapter 26 Unappreciated, 01-07-19

9:56pm

To Perfect:

We kissed last Friday and I couldn't have imagined a better moment with you, in your arms as you pull me close to you. You were afraid all this time that I wouldn't like you back, but I too feared the same. Your kisses feel like delicate roses and taste sweeter than palm sugar; at this moment I crave you. The more I think about you or our moment together the more I believe in our destiny together. I may just be creating a little perfect world in my mind, but I feel inside my very heart and soul that I love you already. Your insecurities do not define you as much as you think they do; I accept and love all of them. I told you that I felt used by past lovers and most others around me, and you asked me why I thought that; I didn't have a coherent answer until later that night. I felt unappreciated by them and thus I felt used because they took a part of me without even acknowledging the pedestal that I put them on in my life. I don't want to be or feel used or unappreciated by you; that would hurt more than the others combined. I love you. Please realize my worth.

Chapter 27 Forbidden Love, 06-26-19

12:28am

To Perfect:

My heart always goes to you as if it's supposed to mean something. All I feel now is love for you; lost love in specific. I keep telling myself that I fell in love with the wrong person, but is this really what it's supposed to feel like? I love you so much Perfect, and I hate that we're apart. I hate that you chose your own comfort over commitment with me. I hate that you can easily shut off your emotions when you want to. I hate that you're not with me right now. "Maybe it's just the wrong time". Well I sure hope it is. I don't know what I'd do with myself if I didn't marry you. I love you so much and I'm typing this as I cry. I only cry when I experience true pain, and the pain of not having you with me is enough to send streams down my cheeks. I love you so much. I say "I love you" instead of "I miss you". I feel like I've been avoiding my true feelings for you for so long. I love you so much Perfect, and I'll never stop loving you. I pray that you find your way back to me, somehow, some way, some day. I won't stay waiting for you, but I will prioritize you when the time comes. I love you so much, and I feel pain from loving you this hard, this intensely. I hope you feel the same way about me. I hope that our paths will cross again just so that I can look into your beautiful amber eyes again and tell you how much I love you. Everything in me wants to visit you, but I know that it's best if we keep our distance. I love you so much and I'll never stop loving you. You'll always be a piece of me. I love you so much and I want all of you. I love you so much and I wish that you were here to comfort me as I type this. I just need one hug, one loving glance, one kiss to piece me back together. My self worth is not in you, it is in myself, but I consider you a part of me. You've helped me grow so tall and mighty in myself and I hope that I've done the same for you. I love you so much and I can't wait to see you again.

Chapter 28 Finished, 01-13-20

2:17am

To Perfect:

I just want to say that you were right, about everything. You do need to distance yourself from me and you do need to lose that part of yourself that love-loves me. I'm too much for you. You want me to be cute and small and soft spoken and agreeable. But I'm not. I mean, I am cute and small and soft spoken when I want to be, and agreeable if I agree on the matter, but I'm not so simple. You said it yourself, I'm passionate and "crazy", and that I have a way with words when I write. I don't know why you expected so little from me at first; if anything I hurt you more than you hurt me because you know that you'll never be enough for me. You said it yourself, that I have all these plans for my life and all these ambitions; you know that you won't be able to keep track or keep up. That's ok, we're different people living different lives, just like everyone else. I don't want to expect more from you than what you're capable of. I'm not crazy or stupid or naive, just finding my way through life the best I can. You know how much pain you put me through, the confusion, the heartaches. You know how many times I still forgave you for hurting me. After I left your house back to Pompano, I thought to myself and came to the conclusion that a woman should NEVER have to beg a man for his love. I feel so stupid for having begged you for years when all you wanted was to not get attached. But you still grew feelings and continued to have me doubt my place in your life. I didn't deserve that from you, I deserved love and respect for all that I've done for you, for all that I put up with. There's a quote that goes along the lines of this: the more a woman forgives a man, the more the man falls in love, and when he is at his peak love for this woman, the woman has the least love for him because the more she forgave him, the more she fell out of love with him. I'm done, completely. I don't want to feel bad for accidentally offending you if I tell you a story about my life, and I don't want to have to cry or write anymore stupid stories to you about how much I love you. I probably don't even want to hear from you ever again. I'm done. At least this much is clear to me: that I never want to feel the way with another man like how I felt with you. We had our good times, but that's all they'll ever be to me, good memories. Good memories in the midst of heartache and confusion and tears. I hope the best for your life, sincerely, I just don't want you in mine anymore.

Chapter 29 Not Yet, 03-30-20

9:58pm

To Perfect:

Life is balanced. That's all it is. Not love, not hate, not good or evil. Just balanced. I'm sitting with friends and I'm writing about you. I hope you understand how much you mean to me. I may have intended to want to fall in love with you, but not at first. It happened gradually. I feel like the more I'm alive the more I'll fall in love with you. I've come to normalize this confusion in my life, between you and me. But in reality, it's not confusing. Its love. I want to hold you in my arms and tell you everyday that I love you. I want to hold your hand and kiss it every moment that I can. I want to love you like how old couples love each other after 40-50-60+ years of marriage. A part of me thinks that my love for you is just made up in my mind and that I'm romanticizing everything, but another part of me contradicts that and says that feelings lead you to your truest self, to who you're meant to be. If my real self is loving you then so be it. I've endured heartbreak from you multiple times, and I'll risk being heartbroken again because the feeling of loving you is so much greater than the temporary pain of hatred and confusion. Life is not good or evil, just balanced, and I have to accept that. I hope you can accept that too. I love you and I miss you. Hold me tightly next time we meet, if we have that privilege. Kiss me passionately and show me your love like how I've shown mine. There's a reason why I still love you. There's a reason why I keep writing to you, even after years of saying that "I'm done". I love you. Please don't take my love for granted. Only God knows if you'll ever find a love like mine again.

Chapter 30 I Found You, 08-17-20

1:55pm

To The One:

I found you but you found me first. I only came to realize I found you when I saw that everything I ever wanted in a man has manifested inside of you. You found me first because you looked at me first. I never knew life could be so wonderful. I didn't know my life needed redemption until I met you. Everything you do seems to redeem a past wrong in my life. Everything you do reminds me of a part of myself that I lost years ago, but found again in you. You've never hurt me (knowingly), and you've never touched me in a way that I never liked; I love your touch. You are exactly how I wanted my true love to be, physically, mentally, and emotionally. My stone wall for me to fall back on, to protect me, and to keep me safe. A strong mind in which the body follows willingly and with purpose. A hardened man to the world but a sweet boy in my presence. You make me feel like a little girl again, I hope I make you relive your childhood joys too. What I lack, you are strong in, and what I am strong in, you lack.

We always help each other, since we met really. I've always felt a connection to you, but I didn't know where the feeling came from. I've never felt so comfortable around someone; you made me feel safe before you were able to keep me safe. Every tear I've wasted on Perfect and all of my past "lovers" have turned into tears of joy whenever I think about you and your care for me; I've felt euphoria once, you were there, but somehow you can make me feel that euphoria when I'm driving home from seeing you or from laying in my bed before I go to sleep. I wake up every morning with the thought of you and how lovely you are — how lovely you've always treated me. A man in every way, my perfect man. A warrior in war, but a father at home, and a lover and comforter when I gaze into your beautiful sky blue eyes. Your eyes have always amazed me: a soul so genuine revealed, and sincerity that could quiet any argument; a gold ring forms around your pupil when the sunlight hits your eyes, and I knew from the first time I saw them that I never wanted to look at any other eyes in the same way that I look at yours; the strength and authority in your gaze when you need to stand your ground; I never want to lose your gaze upon mine. Your hair as gold as the ring in your eyes, and so easy to style and to pull. I've always had a thing for blondes. Your kiss on my cheek is so soft for so tough a man you present to the world, as you were raised and taught to do so. You stand tall like I've always imagined, and you know how to talk to me when I'm angry and when I feel like the world is falling apart; you stabilize me. You remember the smallest details about me and about the things I like, and you make an effort everyday to remind me of it. You always smell so nice, even when you don't try to. When you try to smell nice you smell sweeter than the perfume department at Macy's, and when you don't, I'd still rather have your scent than that of the most expensive cologne known to the world; your scent would make the expensive cologne smell better once it's on your skin. You are a man in every way imaginable: in character, in values, in treatment of others, in family, and in strength (both physical and mental). You know me better than I know myself at times, and you always remind me of it in little ways everyday. I can't believe that I didn't notice your qualities until after I stormed out that night in disappointment at the start of the month. You've always been there for me and I only realized months later. You've always proved yourself to me, bettering your life because you see how I live mine, and bettering yourself because you want to be better for me. I notice everything. Thank you for being so wonderful to me. This is where my book ends. I didn't know when I'd finish it, but I knew that I would finish it when I felt that the time was right. I started this book with anxiety over a love affair with someone I met at a fair, but I'm finishing it with your sweetness and redemption from the wrongs of that lover and of others. You are slowly fixing a heart that I didn't know was broken. You are taking down borders that seemed like they would never go down. You make me a better person for myself because I see how I can be better for you. You are my missing puzzle piece, my blueberry to my dark chocolate, and my balance in this unbalanced world. I promise to give you all of my love because I know that you will give me all of your love. No secrets between us, no hurt, no heartache. This is true love. Thank you for finding me so quickly.

www.ingramcontent.com/pod-product-compliance
Lightning Source LLC
LaVergne TN
LVHW050420160726
843469LV00041B/1167

* 9 7 8 9 3 5 5 5 9 2 3 4 7 *